The Eating Disorder; The Psychosis; The Person

Emma Bone

BookLeaf Publishing

India | USA | UK

Presentation by *BookLeaf Publishing*

Web: www.bookleafpub.com

E-mail: info@bookleafpub.com

ISBN:9789358319354

First edition 2024

DEDICATION

For Paddy and Mark who taught me the most important lesson of my life; to just live in the moment, not the past, not the future, just now.

ACKNOWLEDGEMENT

Thank you,

To Mrs Angus, for showing kindness in a place barren of the stuff!

To Mary for taking me in and believing there was a person entangled in the mess.

To Nick and Julie for your unwavering support and for bringing music back into my life.

To Bee, Hayley and Donna for being there through the best and the worst.

To everyone in my life now, you have been chosen with care!!

And of course, to Emma M for being the best friend a girl could ever have; and to Carol for enabling such a beautiful friendship to flourish.

PREFACE

After a troubled childhood coping with depression and psychosis she was too young to understand, Emma learnt to cope using an eating disorder and self-harm.

In her late twenties, having exhausted the NHS and been given the labels uncooperative and treatment-resistant, Emma managed to recover, giving up both her coping strategies. This led to a full psychotic breakdown and admission to the local psychiatric ward.

With little therapeutic input but good medical care, a combination of medications was found that worked. Emma was finally free to live her life with music and animals and to achieve her dream of becoming a paramedic.

This book is an attempt to put into words her experience of mental illness, the psychiatric care system and her recovery.

Just Not Hungry

She's the kind of voice you'd love to hate,
But addictions are much stronger
Than anyone cares to admit.

She takes you over
And screws with your mind.
Then spits you out to fend for yourself;
But still she keeps a firm grasp,
Tells you that you want to die.

You're nearly dead anyway,
Because you're

Just Not Hungry

You breathe, you talk,
You starve, you sleepwalk

She eats at your mind,
Screams louder than hell,
She makes sure you know
Just how worthless you really are

But still you listen and obey,
She's stronger than you'll ever be.

Her mind games weaken you every day
But you still believe that you're

Just Not Hungry

That's what she's taught you to say.

Bulimia

You lied to me,
Yet I lied for you,
Kept you hidden
Out of view

Of those who could only
Stop and stare,
But more, from those
Who might have cared.

I lied to hide you,
I lied to feed you,
I stole from those
Who could not see you.

I did become you
And all that you stood for.
Believed that destruction
Was all I was good for.

Bones Scraped Clean

How can you think of me
As so very weak?
Can't you see beyond
My pathetic heartbeat?

Beyond the horror
Of bones scraped clean,
Of blood pressure swooning,
Of eyes that scream?

It takes a lot of strength
To let your bones crumble,
To keep on going
Until your stomach can't rumble.

Fighting the body's instinct to survive,
Seeking and winning control for your mind.

A last ditch attempt
To let the brain succeed,
In a world full of excess,
Too much noise, light and speed.

To slow it all down
You must control your desires,

Stop all your neediness,
Put out the fire.

How is it weak
To eradicate your needs?
Don't need food, don't need friends,
Don't need sleep, don't need men.

If only you could say the same
And not give in to the sins of greed,
Then you would understand the strength it takes
To live a life of bones scraped clean.

Cutting Is Silent

All the chatter,
All the noise,
The revving of engines,
The talking with boys.

It's all too much,
I'm getting out.
There's nowhere to go,
I need to relax.

Can somebody help me,
I won't let you in.
Can somebody save me
You're not getting in.

Deal with it silently,
Put on a smile,
Stop your attention seeking
Spoilt little child.

Is that what you think of me?
Maybe it is.
It's not how it seems in here,
Alone
In my head,

Avoiding your stares,
Your looks of concern
If I say I can't cope
And need to go home.

Cutting is silent
You never need to know.
Then I can cope
And won't need to go.

Addiction

Sitting, falling,
Unconscious and alone
Empty bottles of pain
She no longer has to feel.

Standing, collapsing,
Half-conscious and alone
A belly full of emptiness
Where feelings once were real.

So dead inside
But breathing deep,
Locked in a glass coffin
Just the illusion of sleep.

She wanders through the emptiness
The old dirt track of bones.
Fingers clasping bottles and ribs.
Addiction feels like home.

A Works Conference

Shut up, the noise
It deafens her.
The voices, the people,
She is running scared.

Who is real,
And who is not?
Who is in her mind
And who has she forgot?

Talking, rustling,
She can't hold the tune,
It's falling down around her
Distorting the patterned room.

Too much going on
Too little going in
She can't hold on
She's cracking up
Someone stop the din.

The voices and the pictures
Are growing and closing in,
Concentration and focus
Have gone, she's giving in.

To the madness that surrounds her
That nobody can stop.
She knows that nothing helps her,
She knows she's lost the plot.

Just a Ghost

Why does the noise level
Bother her so,
She used to have patience,
She used to know,

How to adapt
To the room she was in,
How to speak clearly,
How to grin.

When something was funny
She'd laugh out loud,
Now she forgets,
Always under the cloud,

She's fading away
From the world outside,
Far from the people
Who think she's alive.

She cannot lift her head up
Or put her shoulders down,
She cannot make eye contact,
She cannot help but frown.

She's driving far away from her,
The ones she loves the most,
She can't believe they care for her
When she is just a ghost.

Stigma

Chase away the demons
My time is running out,
They're closing in around me
And I cannot make a sound,

One sound out of my mouth
Will have people think I'm mad.
Keep it buttoned girl,
Just have them think you're sad.

The stigma of depression
Is getting easier to bare,
Say you're hearing voices though
And they'll put you over there,

To a place where people watch you
In short, sharp glimpses of fear.
To a place where you're stood next to them
When in truth you're nowhere near.

So button down the hatches
And cut where they can't see
Deal with the abuse and distortion,
Just deal with it silently.

Faceless Voice

He takes away my words and won't let me speak
He's louder in the morning and likes to give me
grief,
He tells me what others are thinking, but often
gets it wrong,
He tells me I'm not good enough, he tells me I'm
not strong.

His voice is low, and loud, and scary, he often
gives me a fright.
He turns up unexpectedly, like the phantom of
the night.
At times he leans right over me, his speech will
wake me up.
At times he leaves me alone for days, and waits
for me to screw up.

He tells me I'm not welcome, they don't want me
around,
He tells me I'm lazy, a liar and a thief, different
from the crowd,
He berates me for fooling people, pretending
that I care,
When really I'm a selfish bitch, he has me
running scared.

That people will find out the truth and realise I'm
a fraud.
He says he will always protect me if I listen to
his word.
His word can be confusing though, when he
talks about others' thoughts,
And when he takes mine from me and tells me
I'll get caught,

He tells me my motivations after I've committed
the crime,
When I think I'm obeying and doing what's
right, he says I'm out of line,
Whatever I do has an underlying cause, and my
motives are never pure.
He tells me that I'm cruel and bad, so I stay
behind my door.

My Mind is Safe

Men in charge
To hold the keys.
Men who can hurt
But only my body.

My mind is safe,
It's locked away,
I'll keep it there
Through every day.

No one will find it
To get a grip,
Of the tortures it holds,
My mask won't slip.

You won't get in to hurt it,
There isn't any choice,
Not because I don't trust you,
But because I do not trust my voice.

I keep my mind safe
By telling lies,
By hurting my body,
By closing my eyes.

Hallucinations

Feeling better but far from sleep,
These thoughts are coming in
Swirling in her bloodstream,
Creating a centrifuge spin.

Her head is holding tightly
To the pillow, eyes forced shut,
She cannot smile so brightly
When the bad man calls her a slut.

He wakes her from her dreaming
So she fears each sleeping hour
In case he wakes her surprisingly
And controls her with his power.

Three children she sees in the doorway

Holding hands, like a paper chain
That she used to make in childhood,
A distraction from the pain.

Happy, smiling children,
At least that's better than before,
When she saw the girl with chestnut hair
And called her a dirty whore.

Nothing

No will to write,
No will to please,
No will to care for anything,
No will to find complete.

Nothing left to live for,
You took it on the run.
Nothing there to live for,
It left a girl undone.

No one there to find her,
She's lost, far out to sea,
Bobbing silently on the waves,
Planning her final release,

To end it all and kill the shell
The illusions of this girl
Who left so silently, long ago,
That nobody could tell.

The Keychain

They hold the power of your mind
On their keychain.
It jingles and it jangles,
And it deafens those around.
They decide if you feel well
Or if you're poorly,
Some will give you peace of mind
Others like the power,
Of saying no, you all must suffer
From delusions and the pain.
Watching life around you
Whilst you sit alone and fade
Into a world of demons
Tearing at your soul,
They could stop those demons
But their keys are tightly held.
They will not give you medicine,
They will not give you time,
Their podgy little fingers
Holding the fragments of your mind.

Crazy

Crazy dreams of a crazy girl,
What is crazy in this world?

Is it the man who talks at length
To no one who's listening, sat on a bench?

Or is it the woman with staring eyes
Who rocks and dribbles and silently dies?

Or is it the boy who keeps it all in
Then jumps from a bridge knowing he can't
swim?

Or is it the girl you sit next to every day
Who pretends to herself that everything's okay?

You'll never know what crazy means,
Until you've been there, then it never leaves.

Obsession

Mental illness and self-obsession,
Do the two go hand in hand?
I don't have a care for the outside world,
For my friends who can't understand,

What it feels like to cut through flesh,
To be so lost in your head,
To not see the destruction you leave behind
As you crash and burn, so selfish, unkind.

Or is that just unfairly blaming
An illness of the mind?
It's me who should take responsibility
For friends who have been so kind.

So stay alive and look outside
Be aware and read the signs.
Care for others and don't get lost
In the obsessions of your mind.

Just Be Yourself

A day that started out so well
Ended in a heap.
My head is spinning sideways
And I cannot move or speak.

In fact I've spoken well today
And even smiled and laughed.
But now it feels so wrong because
That is not who I am.

When is pretending a good thing,
Something you have to do,
So that others feel much better
And don't get dragged down by you?

And when should you listen to those who say
"Just be yourself today"?
I often think it's alright for you,
Your self is okay.

Missing You

I gaze across the water
And wonder what's on my mind.
There's a nagging feeling
In the back of my head
That keeps me from feeling alive.

So much to live for
When once there was none
And yet I can't quite breathe and be,
When you, my dear, are gone.

Did I kill you with my pacifying pleas?
My lack of sympathy?
When all you needed was a touch of kindness,
I had no empathy.

Off I went to live my life,
Leaving you behind,
And now I miss your beautiful face
The same way you missed mine.

Dear Grannie

25

Thank you and I love you,
Little words that mean a lot.
I hope you're living peacefully
In a world where dementia is not.

You taught me such a lot of things,
How to love, stand up and belong.
In a world that was not made for me
You made it safe, you made me strong,

And now it is time to say goodbye
Although this is not the end,
You live in every breath I breathe,
A Grannie and a friend.

The Red Room

I saw,
I heard,
And I cannot recall.
The names,
The words,
We spoke of nothing at all.

Three people,
Alone
In a warm red room.
Speaking,
Staring,
I remember shadows in the gloom.

Distant memories
Of a forgotten time.
A time that passed me by
As I restore my broken mind.

Little Girl

Recovered but on the edge,
Trying to find herself,
The screaming that she does,
She cannot face herself.

The last remaining demons
Placed deep within her soul,
Locked in a box she can't set free,
For fear of a little girl.

A little girl she hated
For all those years spent on the run,
A little girl who tried her best
Not to come undone.

As an adult now,
She tries to stand up tall,
But still can't face the demons
That haunt that little girl.

Recovered but on the edge,
Trying to find herself,
The screaming that she does,
She cannot face herself.

Robin Song

The robin starts his singing
And you do not mind his song.
He tells you off for smoking
And you know he isn't wrong.

He tells you all the good things
That wait outside locked doors.
He's seen it all and knows there's more
Than your life behind these walls.

Then he flies away,
Off to another lonely soul.
You know you must go home now,
The robin sings your goal.